What's inside...

page 4

page 20

page 10

5L

D0353202

70002738203X

Editor: Karen Brown. Designers: Darren Miles/Charlotte Reilly.
Model Maker: Susie Johns. Artist: Mary Hall.

CASTLE BIN!

1 Cut a rectangle from bendy cardboard measuring 63cm x 34cm. Roll it in to a cylinder and tape in place. Cut a circle of card for the base (about 19cm in diameter) and tape to the bottom.

2 Snip into the top of the cylinder with scissors at intervals of 3.5cm and about 3cm deep. Fold back each alternative flap and tape down.

3 To make the soldiers, use plastic bottles. Stick a crumpled ball of newspaper to the top of each to form a head. On top of this, stick a piece of toilet roll tube. Pad the hat out with scrunched up paper and add a thick fold of paper to the side of the roll to create the hat's feather.

4 Cover the castle and soldiers with 4 layers of papier maché and leave them to dry.

5 Paint the castle grey all over and then add details. Make a flag from tissue paper stuck to a straw. Paint the soldiers with smart red jackets and black trousers and hats.

YOU WILL NEED:

Bendy cardboard, scissors, two plastic bottles, toilet roll tube, newspaper, sticky tape, PVA glue, paints, coloured tissue paper, straw.

5

ELE-FANTASTIC!

Elephants are often used during festivals and celebrations in Asia. They are decorated with flowers, ornaments and patterned covers. Have a go at decorating your own elephant, making it as grand and as brightly coloured as you want.

1 Start by tracing off the elephant on the opposite page. Draw it onto thick white paper or thin card.

2 Use your imagination to decorate the elephant as brightly as you can, use glitter glue, three-dimensional paints, sequins or anything else that you can find to decorate the coverings and chains.

3 Now carefully cut it out and mount it on a piece of coloured card.

Make lots of differently decorated elephants and hang them around your bedroom to make a wall border. Attach each one b sticking the tail of the one in front to the trunk of the one behin (Ask an adult before you stick anything to the wall.)

YOU WILL NEED:

Plastic bottle, sand, newspaper, sticky tape, scrap card, PVA glue, paints, black marker pen.

2 Now twist newspaper into sausage shapes and attach it to the sides of the bottle with sticky tape to form arms. Scrunch newspaper into balls to build up the feet.

3 Roll up newspaper for the head. Attach smaller rolls of paper for the eyebrows, mouth and nose. Attach the head to the body. Cover with five layers of torn paper pasted on with PVA glue.

4 When completely dry and rock hard, you can paint it. Finally, use black marker pen to add horrible looking scars!

MAKE ONE OF YOUR FAVOURITE CARTOON CHARACTERS OR SUPERHEROES INTO A DOORSTOP! FOLLOW THE STEPS FOR FRANKENSTEIN'S MONSTER BUT TAILOR THEM TO YOUR OWN DESIGN. USE PICTURES TO HELP YOU BUILD UP THEIR FEATURES AND PAINT THEM.

KNOCK DOWN

1 To make a pirate, place a crumpled ball of newspaper on top of an empty plastic bottle and tape it firmly in place. For the arms, use pieces of rolled up cardboard.

Choco

2 You can add details to each pirate, to give it a bit of character and individuality. Make a hat or beard from a scrunched up piece of newspaper. Cut a sword from a piece of cardboard.

3 Cover each pirate with three or four layers of torn paper pasted on with PVA glue. Leave them to dry until they're rock hard.

PVA

PIRATES!

4

Meanwhile make the base. Glue a long cardboard tube to a rectangle of cardboard box card. Stick one end of a length of string onto a rubber or paper pulp ball and stick the other end into the top of the tube.

YOU WILL NEED:

Plastic bottles, sticky tape, cardboard, newspaper, PVA glue, string, rubber ball, cardboard tube, paints.

5

Cover with papier maché. When dry, paint the base to look like an island in the sea. Use yellow and orange for the island and when that's dry, paint the sea blue. Then add white for frothy waves. Paint the tube and ball.

6

Paint the pirates. Look at the pirates on this page for ideas on how to dress them. Add eye patches and spotty scarves for that authentic sea dog look!

CREATE A WOOLLY JUMPER BY PAINTING LINES AROUND THE NECK, SLEEVES AND BOTTOM.

TRY PAINTING DETAILS SUCH AS BELTS AND A WAISTCOAT.

PAINT A STRIPY T-SHIRT AND THIN MOUSTACHE!

ADD A SKULL AND CROSSBONES AND A SPOTTY SCARF.

CURLY PICTURES!

CREATE COLOURFUL PICTURES WITHOUT USING PENS OR PAINT. ALL YOU NEED IS SOME DIFFERENT COLOURED PAPER, SOME SCISSORS AND SOME PVA GLUE.

1 Cut your coloured paper into lots and lots of long, narrow strips. (You can actually buy paper already cut into strips like this.)

2 To make the butterfly, I stuck a butterfly shape cut from white paper on to a sturdy card background. Then I curled paper strips into tight and loose spirals and stuck them down.

3 For the flower picture, I stuck the paper curls straight onto the card background. To make the petal and leaf shapes, curl the paper, loosen it a bit and then pinch one side before sticking down.

YOU CAN MAKE PICTURES OR GREETINGS CARDS - TRY IT YOURSELF!

13

THINGS TO DO WITH

Create some wrinkly Art Attacks using corrugated paper or card. You can find corrugated card in cardboard boxes or you can buy it from craft shops.

CORRUGATED CASE!

MAKE A COOL FOLDER TO KEEP YOUR ART ATTACK DRAWINGS IN.

Cut two rectangles of corrugated card, one longer than the other, and cut a rounded edge around each piece.

Place the long rectangle on a table with the smaller piece on top. The corrugated sides should be on the outside. Hold them together as you punch holes round the edges and thread with string. Fold the longer bit down to form a flap. Punch two holes in the flap (as illustrated), then glue a length of string in place behind the flap to the front of the folder, make sure there is enough string to thread through the flaps and tie the folder shut.

PENCIL POT!

A UNIQUE CONTAINER FOR YOUR PENS, PENCILS AND PAINT BRUSHES.

Use coloured corrugated card or paper to decorate an empty cardboard snack tube. Stick the ridged paper around the outside and on the inside.

Or you can use plain corrugated card and then paint it. Not only does it give a great looking texture but the ridges make it easy to bend around the container.

I finished the pot off with a foam flower but you could make decorations from anything you like.

CORRUGATED CARD!

CRINKLE CARDS!

SEND A MESSAGE WITH A CORRUGATED COLLAGE CARD.

Corrugated card or paper is perfect for making collages as well.

Here I've created some fantastic birthday cards! If you don't have any coloured corrugated card, simply get some ordinary ridged card from a cardboard box and paint it.

Sketch out your idea for a greetings card or picture first then cut out pieces of different coloured card and use paper glue to layer them onto a bigger piece of folded card.

CROWNING GLORY!

CORRUGATED CARD STOPS YOU FROM GOING ROUND THE BEND!

Corrugated card is used in boxes because it is strong but lightweight. Use it to make strong foundations for your papier maché models.

It's also useful for making curved shapes. Bend corrugated card with the ridges running from top to bottom - perfect for shapes like this crown.

COLOURFUL CLOWN!

PHOTOCOPY OR TRACE THE CLOWN PICTURE TO HAVE AN ART ATTACK!

YOU WILL NEED
Card, glue, paints, glitter glue, black permanent marker.

DECORATE THE CLOWN ANY WAY YOU WISH! I PAINTED
MY CLOWN AND WHEN IT WAS DRY, I EDGED
EVERYTHING WITH BLACK PEN.

HOW ABOUT DECORATING THE CLOWN WITH BITS OF
PAPER CUT FROM MAGAZINES, SCRAP FABRIC, FOIL ETC?
GO FOR A CLOWN COLLAGE!

WHAT ABOUT STICKING THE
CLOWN TO THE FRONT OF
A FOLDED PIECE OF
COLOURED CARD TO MAKE
A GREETINGS CARD?

Poster
Paint

FAKE CAT FLAP!

FIX THIS FUNNY CAT FLAP TO THE BOTTOM OF A DOOR!

1 Cut out two rectangles of thick card measuring 21cm x 23cm. Cut a smaller rectangle out of one of the pieces leaving a frame 1.5cm wide. Stick them together.

2 To make the cat's head, start with a crumpled ball of paper, bound tightly with sticky tape. Make the muzzle from small pieces of cardboard, taped together. Then add cardboard ears.

3 Make the cat's shoulders from a tube of card with the end snipped. Stick this to the centre of the card, then tape the head on. Roll a sheet of newspaper to make a leg and tape to one side of the shoulders.

4 Cover the model with three to four layers of torn kitchen paper pasted on with diluted PVA glue. Leave it to dry until rock hard.

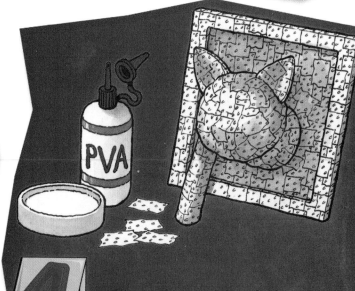

5

Paint the cat's body in the same
colour as black and white, or up to you.
Paint the eyes too. Finally, add some whiskers
made from a few pipe cleaners or bristles
snipped from a broom and glued in place.

-19-

THE LAST STRAW!

HOW ABOUT MAKING A LARGE SCARECROW FOR THE GARDEN OR A SMALL ONE FOR A WINDOW BOX? HERE'S HOW...

1 Start by covering a balloon with four layers of papier maché. Leave it to dry.

PVA

2 Meanwhile, make the hat. Find a bowl that fits on top of the balloon. Stand it on a piece of cardboard and draw around it. Then draw another circle outside this circle to make a brim. Cut it out.

3 Put this cardboard ring over the bowl. Cover the bowl with cling film. Then cover the bowl and ring with four layers of papier maché and leave it to dry.

PVA

20

4 Burst the balloon and remove the pieces. Cut a hole large enough to fit the broom handle or cardboard tube. Push the handle inside the papier maché shell and secure with sticky tape.

5 Make a card cone for the nose and tape in place. Tape two long cardboard tubes on for arms.

6 Cover the whole thing with three layers of papier maché and leave to dry.

7

Paint the head and add a face. Stick on straw or rafia for hair. Also stick it round the hands and neck.

8

Dress the scarecrow in an old shirt. After painting the hat, stick it on the head.

SUPER STRAWS

USE COLOURED STRAWS TO MAKE SOME EX-STRAW-DINARY ART ATTACKS!

From pictures..

..and frames

..to whiskers..

..and chains!

YOU CAN ALSO USE STRAWS TO BUILD PAPIER MACHÉ MODELS AND MAKE BLOW PAINTINGS!

JELLYFiSH PLATES!

HOW ABOUT THESE FOR A QUICK AND JELLY-TASTIC ART ATTACK!

YOU WILL NEED:

Paper plate, tissue paper, paints, glue or staples

1 Cut a paper plate in half and paint each half in a different colour. I used pink and blue.

2 When they are dry, paint the straight edge in the opposite colour.

3 Use black and white paints to add facial details.

4 Take a big piece of tissue and fold it in half. Cut lots of curved narrow strips into it leaving a 2cm margin at the top.

5 Glue or staple the strips to the straight edge of the plate, at the back. Use one strip to make a hook.

INSTEAD OF TISSUE, USE SHINY PAPER. THIS GIVES IT UNDERWATER SPARKLE!

CHUNKY COVERS!

Choose a book with a thick strong cover. (You could always stick a piece of thick card to the front of a book with a thinner cover.) Draw an outline of a simple shape on the front using a felt tip pen.

GIVE A PLAIN OLD BOOK A NEW LOOK WITH THESE CRAZY CHUNKY COVERS! CREATE YOUR OWN 3 DIMENSIONAL DESIGNS.

Scrunch up small bits of kitchen roll, dip in a diluted PVA glue mixture and stick them onto the book cover, filling in the shape you have drawn. Smooth over with your finger tips.

Leave it to dry until rock hard. Then paint with bright colours. When the paint is dry, add details with black marker pen. When that's dry, 'varnish' by painting it with a coat of PVA glue.

HOT TIPS!

Wait until the cover is dry, then outline everything with black marker pen - it will make it stand out!

Keep your designs simple, they will be more effective.

Personalise diaries, address books and photo albums with your chunky cover designs. But don't use a library or a school book.

Be careful not to soak the cover when you are using the wet kitchen roll. The cover will bend if it becomes too wet.

HERE'S A GREAT IDEA FOR AN ART BOOK!

INVITE IDEAS!

HAVING A PARTY? TRY THESE FOR UNIQUE, FUN INVITATIONS! THEY HAVE REMOVABLE BALLOONS OR MASKS TO GET YOUR GUESTS IN THE PARTY MOOD!

oink! oink!

YOU CAN MAKE ALL SORTS OF ANIMAL INVITATIONS WITH THIS IDEA!

EAR THIS!

1 Fold a piece of card in half. Cut a pig's face from pink card and stick it to the front.

2 Cut a nose shape from the card and stick it to the face with a piece of cardboard in between to make it stand out.

3 Draw a face on your pig and stick on googly eyes.

4 Make holes where the ears would be and poke a pink balloon through each one.

EYE EYE!

1 Draw an eye mask onto card and cut it out. Cut the eye holes out as well.

2 Decorate the mask with glitter, sequins and feathers.

3 Fold a piece of card in half and then stick the mask on the front with a piece of sticky tack. (You want the mask to be removable.)

4 Write a message on the front.

fancy dress PARTY!

MAKE LOADS OF DIFFERENT MASKS FOR YOUR INVITATIONS!